YOUR BRAIN WHEN YOU'RE SAD

BY ABBY COLICH

T0014932

BLUE OWL
BOOKS

TIPS FOR CAREGIVERS

Social and emotional learning (SEL) helps children manage emotions, learn how to feel empathy, create and achieve goals, and make good decisions. One goal of teaching SEL skills is to help children understand what is going on in their bodies and brains when they experience certain emotions. The more children understand, the more easily they may be able to regulate their emotions and empathize with others.

BEFORE READING

Talk to the readers about what makes them feel sad and how they react to this emotion.

Discuss: Think about a time when you felt sad. What did you do?

AFTER READING

Talk to the readers about what happens in their brains when they feel sad.

Discuss: What parts of the brain are at work when you are sad? What is one way you can help yourself feel better?

SEL GOAL

Children may struggle with processing their emotions, and they may lack accessible tools to help them do so. Explain to children that changes take place in their brains when they feel strong emotions. These changes can affect how their bodies feel. Certain actions can trigger changes in the brain that help them feel better.

TABLE OF CONTENTS

CHAPTER 1
What Is Sadness? 4

CHAPTER 2
Sadness in Your Brain 8

CHAPTER 3
It's OK to Feel Sad 16

GOALS AND TOOLS
Grow with Goals 22
Try This! 22
Glossary 23
To Learn More 23
Index 24

WHAT IS SADNESS?

Have you ever felt left out? Maybe someone teased you. Or maybe you lost someone close to you. These are all tough situations.

When these things happen, we often feel sad. Sadness is an **emotion**. It is a normal **reaction** when you feel hurt or left out or experience a loss.

You may get a lump in your throat and want to cry. Your chest might feel tight. You might frown or have a sad look on your face. You may slump over and feel tired.

Your body feels this way because your brain is working hard. It is helping you **process** how you feel.

SADNESS VS. DEPRESSION

Sadness eventually goes away. Depression lasts a long time. People with depression may be sad. But they may also feel **numb**. They may struggle to feel emotions, such as happiness. If you think you are depressed, talk to a trusted adult.

CHAPTER 2

SADNESS IN YOUR BRAIN

Your brain is a control center. It processes emotions. Scientists are still studying exactly what happens in our brains when we are sad.

Scientists studied people's brains while they looked at photos that made them sad. They saw that the amygdala was at work.

Up to 70 different parts of the brain could be involved in processing sadness. The hippocampus is likely one. In one study of sad people, scientists saw the amygdala and hippocampus send messages to each other.

anterior
cingulate
cortex

hippocampus

amygdala

vagus nerve

The anterior cingulate cortex goes to work when you feel **physical** pain. It also works when your feelings get hurt. Scientists think it sends a message to your vagus nerve, which can cause you to feel pain and **nausea**.

A BROKEN HEART

Have you ever heard someone say their heart is broken? Your heart doesn't really break, but sadness can make your chest feel tight or heavy. Scientists think the vagus nerve plays a part in these feelings.

We experience **grief** when we lose someone or something close to us. The brain works extra hard when you are grieving to help you process what happened. This is why grief and sadness can make us feel tired.

A GOOD CRY

Have you ever felt better after crying? This is because your body releases **endorphins** when you cry. This chemical makes you feel good. Also, your tears contain a **protein** that reduces pain.

CHAPTER 3

IT'S OK TO FEEL SAD

Everyone feels sad sometimes. It can help us make sense of what happens around us. Sad feelings don't last forever. If you are sad, think of a time you were happy. Remind yourself you will feel happy again.

Being **mindful** can also help you feel better. Find a comfortable, quiet area. Sit down and take some deep breaths. Focus on your breathing.

Spending time with others can help you feel better, too. It's OK if you want to be alone, but talking to someone can help. When you are with other people, your brain makes a **hormone** called oxytocin. This chemical helps you feel better.

SADNESS AND EMPATHY

When you see someone cry or watch a sad movie, you might feel sad, too. This is **empathy** at work. It means you are relating to how another person is feeling.

Learn what makes you sad. This will help you **manage** your emotions. Go for a walk or read a good book. See if you can learn what helps you feel better!

GOALS AND TOOLS

GROW WITH GOALS

Understanding that changes take place in your brain can help you feel better when you are sad.

Goal: Remember, it is OK to be sad sometimes. Everyone gets sad once in a while. Keep this in mind. It will help you process your sadness and know that you will feel better.

Goal: Be mindful. Slow down and pay attention to what is around you. This can help train your brain to stay calm when you are upset.

Goal: Reflect on a time when you felt sad. Did you feel better later? Remember this the next time you are sad. You will feel better again.

TRY THIS!

Journaling can help you process your feelings. The next time you are sad, write down what happened, why you think you may be sad, and how you are feeling. Try to name any other feelings you have, like disappointment, frustration, hurt, or rejection. If you don't like writing, try drawing or creating something to help you process your feelings.

GLOSSARY

emotion
A feeling, such as happiness, sadness, or anger.

empathy
The ability to understand and be sensitive to the thoughts and feelings of others.

endorphins
Substances created by the brain that reduce pain and cause pleasant feelings.

grief
A feeling of great sadness or deep distress.

hormone
A chemical substance made by your body that affects the way your body grows, develops, and functions.

manage
To succeed in something that is difficult.

mindful
A mentality achieved by focusing on the present moment and calmly recognizing and accepting your feelings, thoughts, and sensations.

nausea
A feeling of wanting to throw up.

numb
Not being able to feel anything or not being able to react.

physical
Relating to the body.

process
To gain an understanding or acceptance of something.

protein
A type of chemical compound found in all living plant and animal cells.

reaction
An action in response to something.

TO LEARN MORE

FACT SURFER

Finding more information is as easy as 1, 2, 3.

1. Go to www.factsurfer.com

2. Enter "**yourbrainwhenyou'resad**" into the search box.

3. Choose your book to see a list of websites.

INDEX

amygdala 9, 10, 11

anterior cingulate cortex 11, 13

body 7, 14

brain 7, 8, 9, 10, 14, 19

breaths 17

cry 7, 14, 19

depression 7

emotion 5, 7, 8, 20

empathy 19

endorphins 14

heart 13

hippocampus 10, 11

hurt 5, 13

left out 4, 5

loss 4, 5, 14

mindful 17

oxytocin 19

pain 13, 14

scientists 8, 9, 10, 13

teased 4

tired 7, 14

vagus nerve 11, 13

Blue Owl Books are published by Jump!, 5357 Penn Avenue South, Minneapolis, MN 55419, www.jumplibrary.com

Copyright © 2023 Jump! International copyright reserved in all countries. No part of this book may be reproduced in any form without written permission from the publisher.

Library of Congress Cataloging-in-Publication Data

Names: Colich, Abby, author.
Title: Your brain when you're sad / by Abby Colich.
Description: Minneapolis, MN: Jump!, Inc., [2023]
Series: Brainpower | Includes index.
Audience: Ages 7–10
Identifiers: LCCN 2022021489 (print)
LCCN 2022021490 (ebook)
ISBN 9798885241465 (hardcover)
ISBN 9798885241472 (paperback)
ISBN 9798885241489 (ebook)
Subjects: LCSH: Sadness in children–Juvenile literature. | Sadness–Juvenile literature. | Sadness–Physiological aspects–Juvenile literature. | Brain–Juvenile literature.
Classification: LCC BF723.S15 C65 2023 (print)
LCC BF723.S15 (ebook)
DDC 155.4/124–dc23/eng/20220610
LC record available at https://lccn.loc.gov/2022021489
LC ebook record available at https://lccn.loc.gov/2022021490

Editor: Eliza Leahy
Designer: Emma Bersie

Photo Credits: Airdone/Dreamstime, cover; MillaF/Shutterstock, 1; TY Lim/Shutterstock, 3; Pixel-Shot/Shutterstock, 4; SDI Productions/iStock, 5, 12–13; CGN089/Shutterstock, 6–7; Ground Picture/Shutterstock, 8 (doctor); Shutterstock, 8 (computer); zhukovvvlad/Shutterstock, 9 (background); KPG-Payless2/Shutterstock, 9 (photo); Shutterstock, 10–11; Satjawat Boontanataweepol/iStock, 14–15; Khosro/Shutterstock, 16; Elena Medoks/Shutterstock, 17; kali9/iStock, 18–19; Indiapicture/Alamy, 20–21.

Printed in the United States of America at Corporate Graphics in North Mankato, Minnesota.